BACKYARD JUNGLE
SAFARI
OPOSSUMS

Ann Tatlock

PURPLE TOAD
PUBLISHING

Copyright © 2015 by Purple Toad Publishing, Inc. All rights reserved. No part of this book may be reproduced without written permission from the publisher. Printed and bound in the United States of America.

Printing   1   2   3   4   5   6   7   8   9

Backyard Jungle Safari
Gray Squirrels
Opossums
Raccoons
Red Foxes

Publisher's Cataloging-in-Publication data
Tatlock, Ann.
   Opossums / written by Ann Tatlock.
      p. cm.
Includes bibliographic references and index.
ISBN 9781624691003
1. Opossums—Juvenile literature. 2.Virginia opossum—Juvenile literature. 3. Virginia opossum—Development. I. Series : Backyard jungle safari.
   QL737 2015
   599.2

Library of Congress Control Number: 2014945185

eBook ISBN: 9781624691010

ABOUT THE AUTHOR: Ann Tatlock is the author of ten novels. Her works have received numerous awards, including the Silver Angel Award from Excellence in Media and the Midwest Book Award. She lives in the Blue Ridge Mountains of Western North Carolina with her husband, daughter, three Chihuahuas and a guinea pig named Lilly.

PUBLISHER'S NOTE: The information in this book has been researched in depth, and to the best of our knowledge is correct. Although every measure is taken to give an accurate account, Purple Toad Publishing makes no warranty of the accuracy of the information and is not liable for damages caused by inaccuracies.

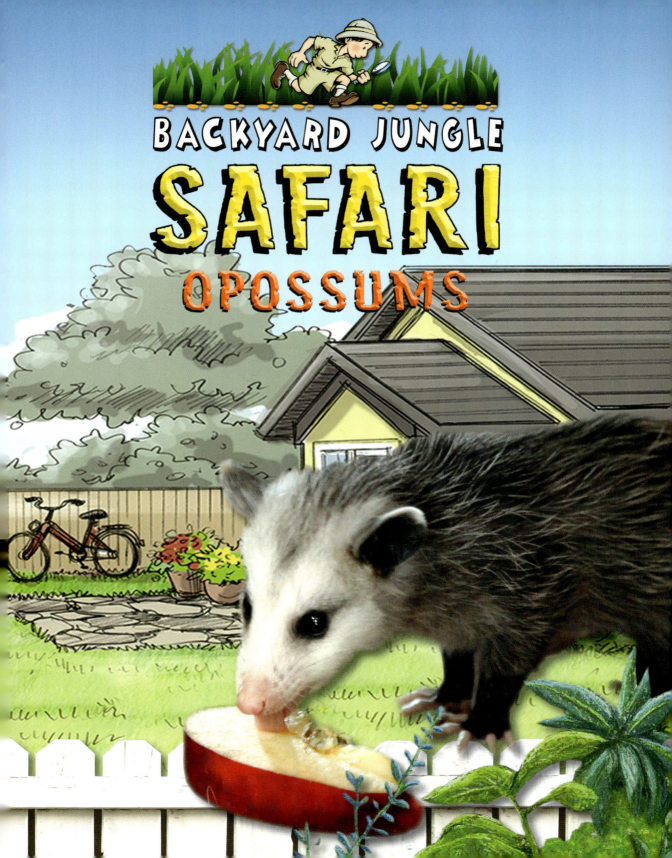

He comes out of the woods, walking low in the grass, trying not to be seen. He heads straight for the garden and begins nibbling on the lettuce. It's an opossum! You know what that means, don't you?

Opossums are nocturnal. They come out at night in search of food. Their eyes have large pupils so they can see in the dark.

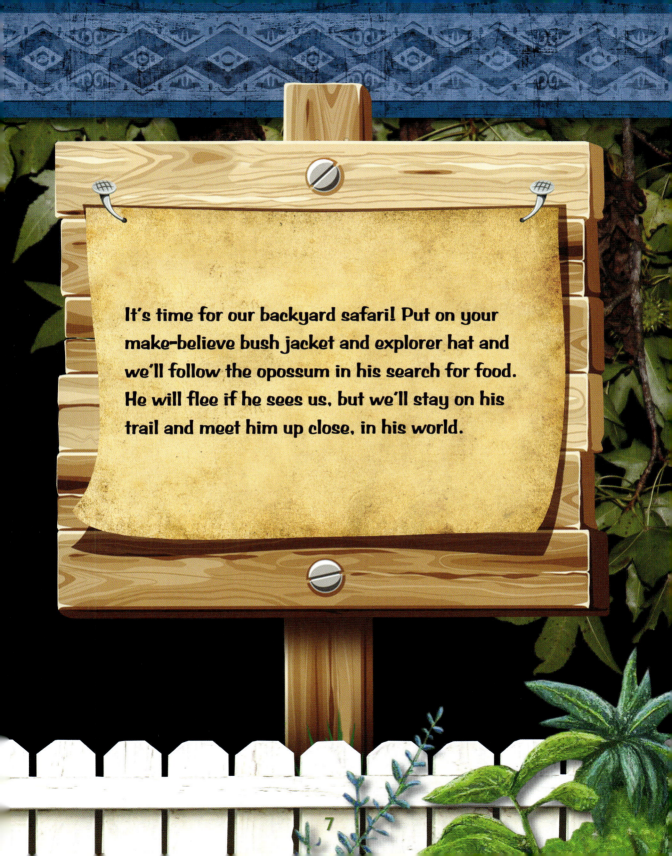

It's time for our backyard safari! Put on your make-believe bush jacket and explorer hat and we'll follow the opossum in his search for food. He will flee if he sees us, but we'll stay on his trail and meet him up close, in his world.

There are more than 60 species of opossums. The little guy eating supper in our garden is a Virginia opossum, the only kind found in North America.

Australian opossum

New Zealand opossum

Virginia opossum

The opossum lives as far south as Nicaragua and as far north as Canada. He has "cousins" in Australasia, a region that includes Australia, Tasmania, and New Zealand.

Opossums journey through woodlands, along streams and even through neighborhoods looking for food. They might travel up to two miles in a night.

They are very quiet, "speaking" only when necessary. Opossums make clicking sounds when calling for a mate and growling, hissing or squawking sounds when threatened by a predator.

Oh, no, we scared him! Look at him scamper up a tree!

The opossum has opposable thumbs on his hind feet and a prehensile tail, both of which help him grasp onto tree branches as he climbs.

Hawk

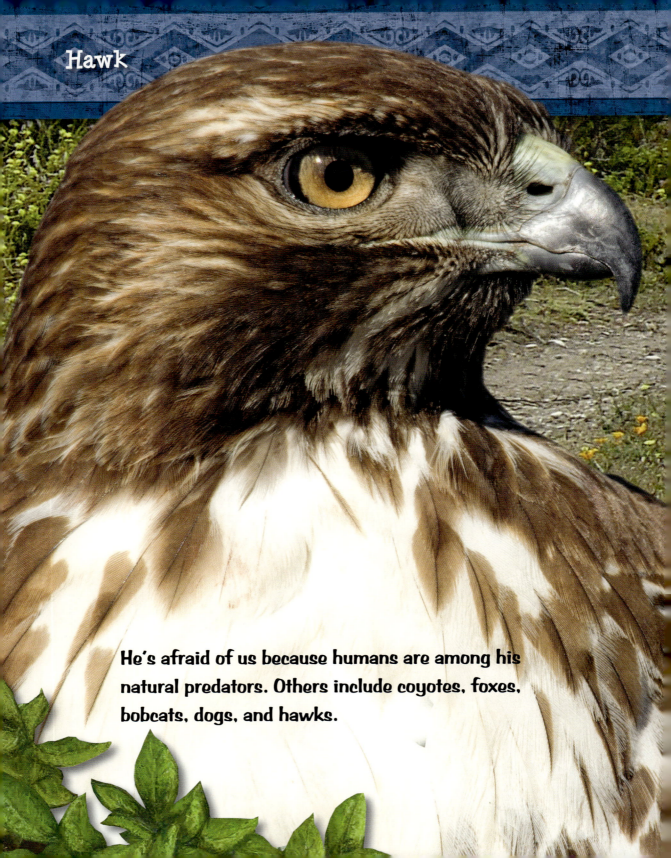

He's afraid of us because humans are among his natural predators. Others include coyotes, foxes, bobcats, dogs, and hawks.

If an opossum isn't killed by a predator first, it will live about two years.

Coyote

The opossum is famous for "playing possum" to ward off attacks. He stiffens and falls, bares his teeth, foams at the mouth, and gives off a terrible odor!

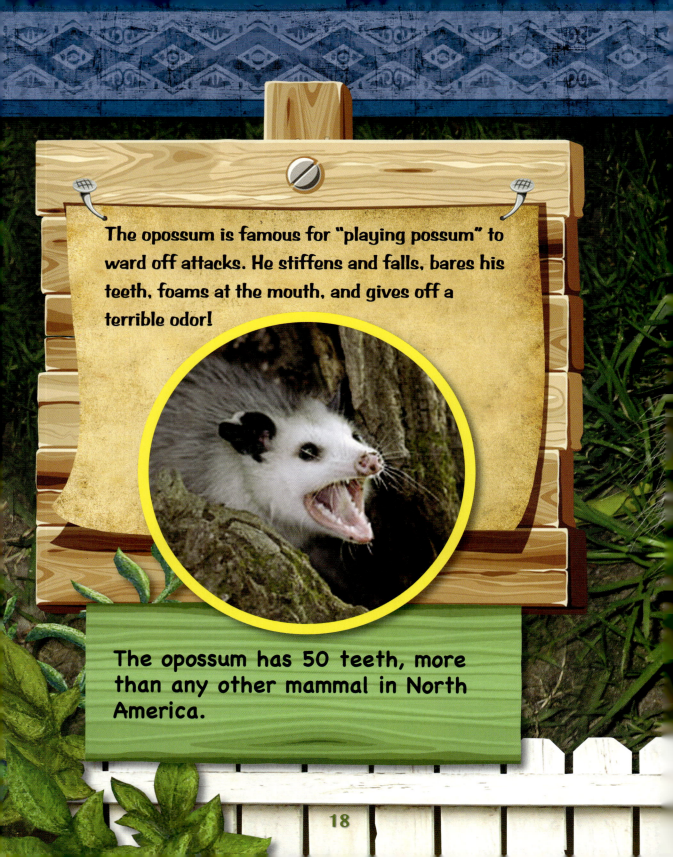

The opossum has 50 teeth, more than any other mammal in North America.

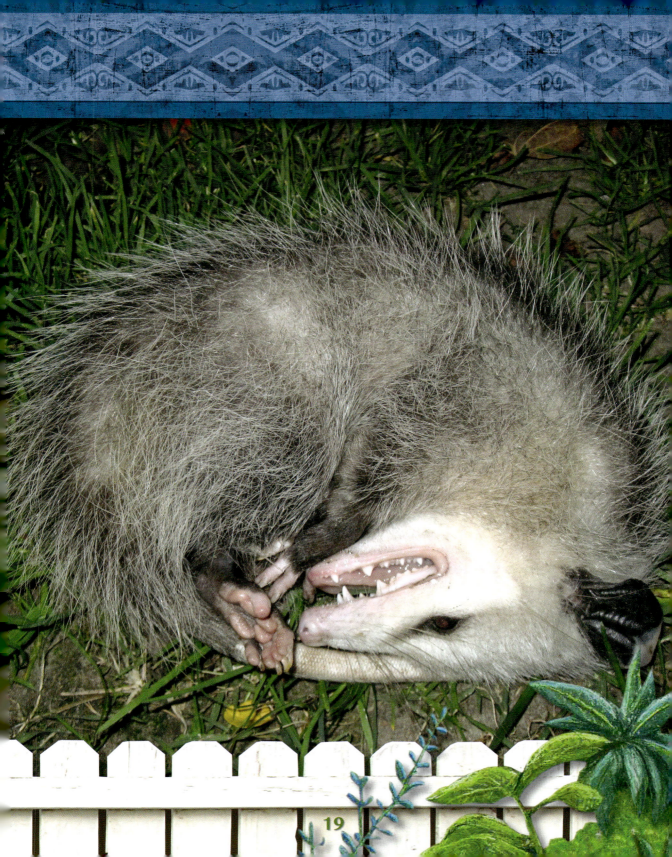

We have interrupted the opossum's dinner. He is known to eat almost anything, including seeds, nuts, fruits, worms, birds, eggs, snakes, insects, garbage, and dead animals!

After eating, the opossum grooms himself like a cat.

The opossum is the only marsupial in North America. That means the female has a pouch for carrying her young.

When the young are born after 13 days gestation, they are no bigger than a honeybee!

Baby →

Right after birth, the tiny babies crawl into their mother's pouch and attach themselves to one of her teats. Mama has enough teats for 13 babies. They will stay in the pouch for two months, just drinking milk and growing.

When full-grown, an opossum is the size of a house cat and can weigh up to 14 pounds.

When the babies are too big to fit in the pouch, Mama Opossum carries them all on her back!

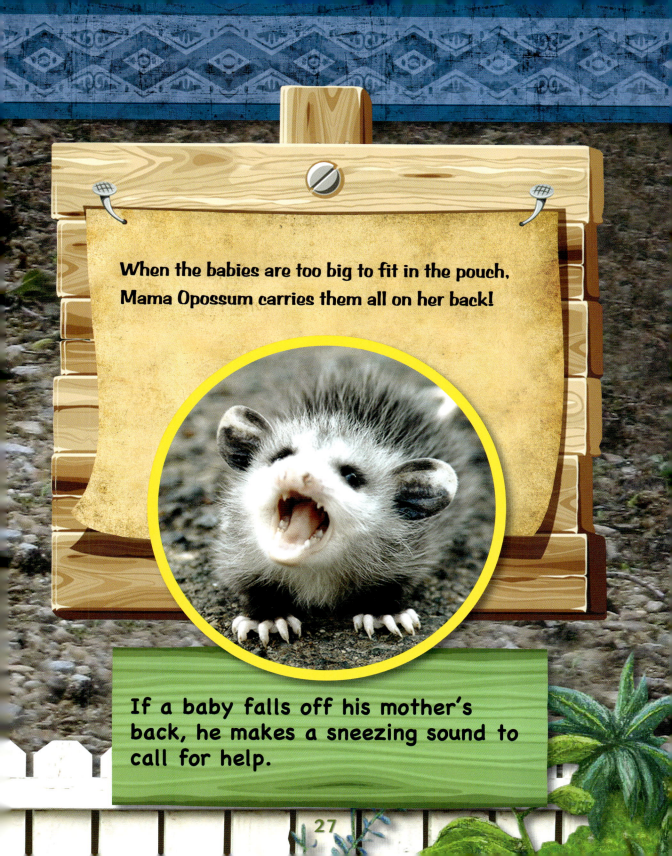

If a baby falls off his mother's back, he makes a sneezing sound to call for help.

After four months, the babies will be big enough to leave their mother. Soon they will have babies of their own!

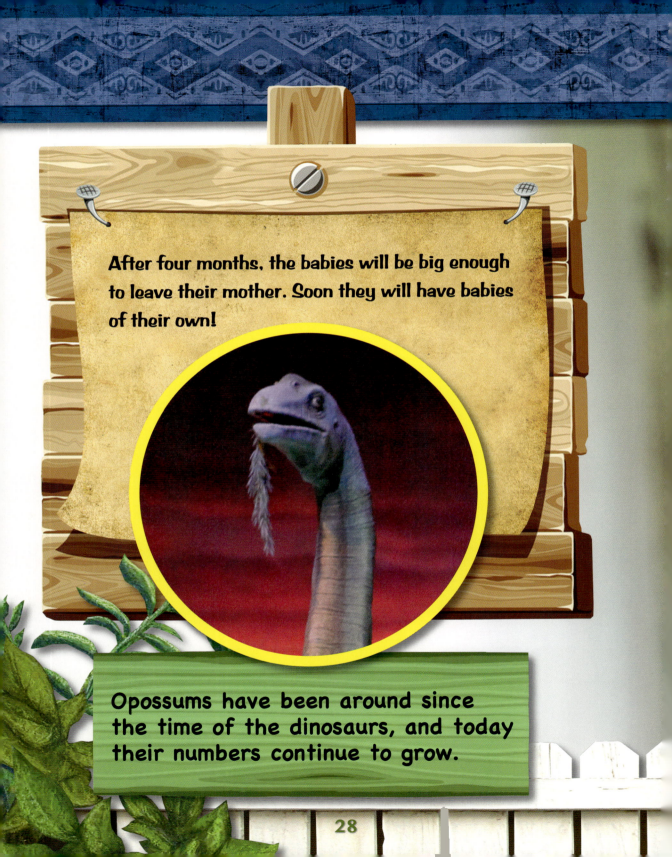

Opossums have been around since the time of the dinosaurs, and today their numbers continue to grow.

When the sun comes up, it will be time for the opossum to go to bed. Opossums sleep in tree holes or abandoned burrows made by other animals, like woodchucks and badgers.

Let's go back inside now so our friend can go on looking for his dinner. Goodbye, Mr. Opossum! Bon appetit!

Contrary to myth, opossums do not hang upside down by their tails while sleeping.

FURTHER READING

Books

Bogue, Gary. *There's an Opossum in My Backyard*. Berkley, California: Heyday Books, 2007.

Green, Emily K. *Opossums (Blastoff! Readers: Backyard Wildlife)*. Minneapolis, Minnesota: Bellwether Media, Inc., 2011.

Linde, Barbara M. *The Life Cycle of an Opossum*. New York: Gareth Stevens Publishing, 2011.

Walker, Sally M. *Opossum at Sycamore Road—A Smithsonian's Backyard Book*. Norwalk, Connecticut: Soundprint, an imprint of Palm Publishing LLC, 2011.

Whitehouse, Patricia. *Opossums (What's Awake?)*. Boston, Heinemann: A division of Houghton Mifflin Harcourt, 2009.

Works Consulted

Beer, Amy-Jane & Pat Morris. *Encyclopedia of North American Mammals,* San Diego: Thunder Bay Press, 2004.

Chinery, Michael, ed. *The Kingfisher Illustrated Encyclopedia of Animals*. New York: Kingfisher Books, 1992.

Reid, Fiona A. *Mammals of North American (Peterson Field Guides)*. New York: Houghton Mifflin Company, 2006.

Spelman, Lucy. *National Geographic Animal Encyclopedia*. Washington D.C.: National Geographic Society, 2012.

Wilson, Don E., & Sue Ruff, eds. *The Smithsonian Book of North American Mammals*. Washington & London: Smithsonian Institution Press, 1999.

On the Internet

National Possum Society
http://www.opossum.org/

INDEX

Australasia 9
Australia 8, 9
badger 31
bobcat 16
burrow 31
Canada 9
clicking 13
coyote 16, 17
dinosaur 28
dog 16
fox 16

gestation 23
groom 20
growling 13
hawk 16
hissing 13
New Zealand 9
Nicaragua 9
nocturnal 6
North America 8, 18, 23
odor 18
opposable 14

playing possum 18
pouch 23, 24, 27
predator 13, 16, 17
prehensile 14
species 8
squawking 13
Tasmania 9
teats 24
woodchuck 31

PHOTO CREDITS: Cover—Graham Higgs; pp. 6-7—Nathan Scott; pp. 8–9—Ryan Somma; pp. 12–13—Gary Owens; pp. 16–17—Joyce Cory; p. 16—Amit Patel; pp. 18–19—Tony Alter; pp. 22–23—Monica R.; pp. 28–29—Ryan Scott; p. 28—Sam Howzit; pp. 30–31—Mike Keeling; all other photos—Public Domain. Every measure has been taken to find all copyright holders of material used in this book. In the event any mistakes or omissions have happened within, attempts to correct them will be made in future editions of the book.